F-35 LIGHTNING IIs

BY DENNY VON FINN

BELLWETHER MEDIA · MINNEAPOLIS, MN

EPIC BOOKS are no ordinary books. They burst with intense action, high-speed heroics, and shadows of the unknown. Are you ready for an Epic adventure?

This edition first published in 2013 by Bellwether Media, Inc.

No part of this publication may be reproduced in whole or in part without written permission of the publisher. For information regarding permission, write to Bellwether Media, Inc., Attention: Permissions Department, 5357 Penn Avenue South, Minneapolis, MN 55419.

Library of Congress Cataloging-in-Publication Data

Von Finn, Denny.
 F-35 Lightning IIs / by Denny Von Finn.
   p. cm. – (Epic : military vehicles)
 Includes bibliographical references and index.
 Summary: "Engaging images accompany information about F-35 Lightning IIs. The combination of high-interest subject matter and light text is intended for students in grades 2 through 7"–Provided by publisher.
 Audience: Grades 2-7.
 ISBN 978-1-60014-885-9 (hbk : alk. paper)
 1. F-35 (Jet fighter plane)–Juvenile literature. I. Title.
 UG1242.F5V656 2013
 623.74'64–dc23

                              2012034022

TABLE OF CONTENTS

F-35 LIGHTNING IIs

THREAT DETECTED

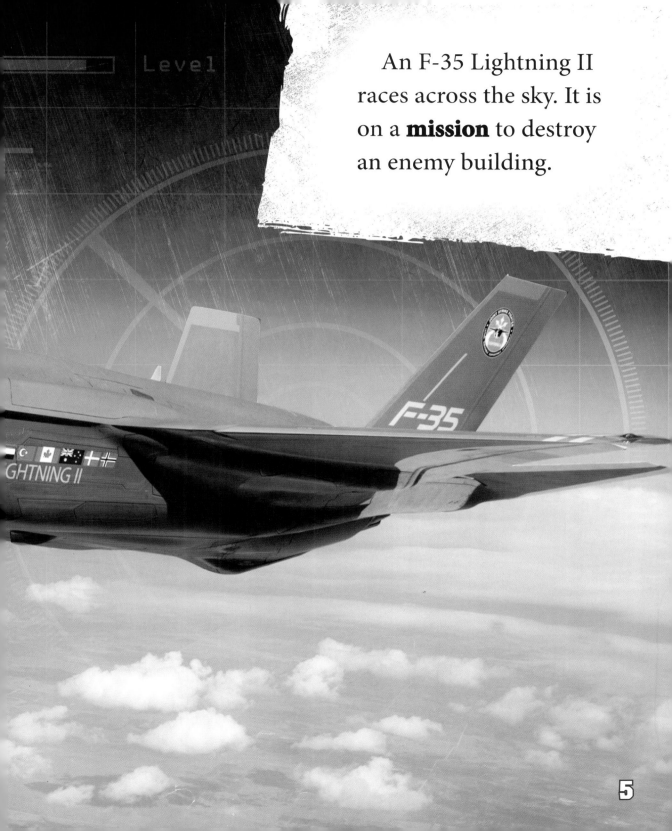

An F-35 Lightning II races across the sky. It is on a **mission** to destroy an enemy building.

Suddenly the F-35's **avionics** warn the pilot of danger. He quickly climbs upward. An enemy rocket sails past.

Then the F-35 finds its target. **Missiles** streak toward the earth. Explosions fill the sky. The enemy was no match for the F-35!

P-38 LIGHTNING

VIT TRANS

TGL

10803 AC

Lightning II Fact

The F-35 was named after the P-38 Lightning. This was a famous U.S. fighter in World War II.

ORDINANCE

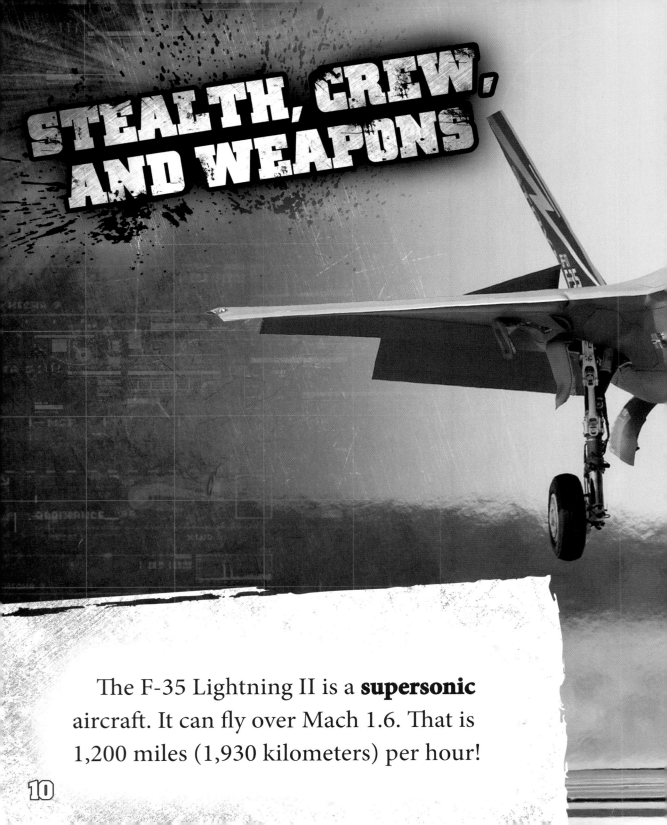

STEALTH, CREW, AND WEAPONS

The F-35 Lightning II is a **supersonic** aircraft. It can fly over Mach 1.6. That is 1,200 miles (1,930 kilometers) per hour!

Lightning II Fact

Some F-35s can hover and land like helicopters.

The F-35 uses **stealth** to sneak past enemy defenses. Its shape helps it **deflect** enemy **radar**.

5

13

0   50

The F-35 pilot sits in the **cockpit**. Cameras outside the aircraft show images on the inside of the pilot's **visor**.

DANGER
EJECTION
SEAT
DANGER

WARNING: DO NOT CUT CANOPY
WITHIN 3 INCHES OF CANOPY FRAME

COCKPIT

RESCUE
EMERGENCY CANOPY
RELEASE ON OTHER SIDE

DANGER
JET
INTAKE
DANGER

0747

TSGT BRIAN WEST

VISOR

Lightning II Fact

The F-35's sensors can find the aircraft's own shadow from 45,000 feet (13,716 meters) in the air!

The pilot uses a **side stick** to fire
the F-35's weapons. The F-35 can
carry several bombs and missiles.
It also has a cannon.

BOMB

SIDE STICK

F-35 MISSIONS

The F-35 is a **multi-role** aircraft. It battles other aircraft in the air. It also destroys targets on the ground. The F-35 even spies on enemies.

VEHICLE BREAKDOWN: F-35 LIGHTNING II

Used By:	U.S. Air Force
	U.S. Marine Corps
	U.S. Navy
Entered Service:	2006
Length:	51.4 feet (15.7 meters)
Height:	14.4 feet (4.4 meters)
Width:	7.1 feet (2.2 meters)
Maximum Takeoff Weight:	70,000 pounds (31,750 kilograms)
Wingspan:	35 feet (10.7 meters)
Top Speed:	about 1,200 miles (1,930 kilometers) per hour
Range:	1,380 miles (2,220 kilometers)
Ceiling:	60,000 feet (18,288 meters)
Crew:	1
Weapons:	25mm cannon, missiles, bombs
Primary Missions:	air-to-air combat, air-to-ground attack

Lightning II Fact

The F-35 will one day replace four U.S. military aircraft. They are the F-16 Fighting Falcon, F/A-18 Super Hornet, A-10 Thunderbolt, and AV-8 Harrier.

More than ten countries plan to use the F-35. This aircraft is sure to keep the world safe for years to come!

GLOSSARY

avionics—electronic systems that help pilots operate aircraft in the sky

cockpit—the area inside an aircraft where the pilot sits

deflect—to cause something to scatter

missiles—explosives that are guided to a target

mission—a military task

multi-role—able to perform more than one task

radar—a system that uses radio waves to locate targets

side stick—a joystick that the pilot uses to fly the aircraft and fire weapons

stealth—an aircraft's ability to fly without being spotted by radar

supersonic—faster than the speed of sound; sound travels about 760 miles (1,225 kilometers) per hour at sea level.

visor—a shield that covers the pilot's face

TO LEARN MORE

At the Library

Alvarez, Carlos. *F-35 Lightning IIs*. Minneapolis, Minn.: Bellwether Media, 2010.

Hamilton, John. *F-35 Lightning II*. Minneapolis, Minn.: ABDO Pub. Co., 2012.

Von Finn, Denny. *Supersonic Jets*. Minneapolis, Minn.: Bellwether Media, 2010.

On the Web

Learning more about F-35 Lightning IIs is as easy as 1, 2, 3.

1. Go to www.factsurfer.com.

2. Enter "F-35 Lightning IIs" into the search box.

3. Click the "Surf" button and you will see a list of related Web sites.

With factsurfer.com, finding more information is just a click away.

INDEX